SLAP. BANG. KISS.

Dan Giovannoni

CURRENCY PRESS
The performing arts publisher

CURRENT THEATRE SERIES

First published in 2022
by Currency Press Pty Ltd,
PO Box 2287, Strawberry Hills, NSW, 2012, Australia
enquiries@currency.com.au
www.currency.com.au

in association with Melbourne Theatre Company.

Typeset by Brighton Gray for Currency Press.
Cover features L-R: Tsungirai Wachenuka, Conor Leach and Sarah Fitzgerald, image by Brett Walker.

Currency Press acknowledges the Traditional Owners of the Country on which we live and work. We pay our respects to all Aboriginal and Torres Strait Islander Elders, past and present.

A catalogue record for this book is available from the National Library of Australia

Contents

SLAP. BANG. KISS. was first produced by Melbourne Theatre Company at the Lawler, Southbank Theatre, Melbourne on 19 April 2022, with the following cast:

SOFIA	Sarah Fitzgerald
DARBY	Conor Leach
IMMI	Tsungirai Wachenuka

Director, Katy Maudlin
Set and Costume Designer, Kate Davis
Lighting Designer, Amelia Lever-Davidson
Composer and Sound Designer, Ian Moorhead

This production of *SLAP. BANG. KISS.* was developed in 2019 and 2020 under the direction of Prue Clark and with the participation of Tahlee Fereday and Artemis Ioannides.

NEXTSTAGE

With a $4.6 million investment by MTC and MTC's Playwrights Giving Circle, the NEXT STAGE Writers' Program has introduced the most rigorous playwright commissioning and development process ever undertaken by the Company, setting a new benchmark for play development in Australia.

Thank you to MTC's Playwrights Giving Circle — its donors, foundations and organisations — for sharing our passion and commitment to Australian stories and Australian writers.

Louise Myer and Martyn Myer AO, Maureen Wheeler AO and Tony Wheeler AO, Christine Brown Bequest, Allan Myers AC QC and Maria Myers AC, Tony Burgess and Janine Burgess, Dr Andrew McAliece and Dr Richard Simmie, Larry Kamener and Petra Kamener

NAOMI MILGROM FOUNDATION

DAN GIOVANNONI's plays for families, young people and adults have been produced across Australia in theatres, school halls, parks, tents and even a barn outside Hobart. Plays include *The Great Un-Wondering of Wilbur Whittaker* (2022), *HOUSE* (2021), *Mad as a Cute Snake* (2019), *Air Race* (2018), *Bambert's Book of Lost Stories* (2016), *Jurassica* (2015), *Cut Snake* (2011) and two adaptations of Christos Tsiolkas' writing, *Merciless Gods* (2018) and *Loaded* (2020). He has won three Green Room Association awards—for *Loaded, Merciless Gods* and *Jurassica*—and *Bambert's Book of Lost Stories* won a Helpmann award for Best Presentation for Children, and was nominated for Best New Australian Work. He was an inaugural writer-in-residence at Melbourne Theatre Company as part of the NEXT STAGE writers' program, where he was commissioned to write *The Body* and *SLAP. BANG. KISS.* A graduate of NIDA, Dan lives on Wurundjeri country in Melbourne with his husband, daughter and two dogs.

CHARACTERS

IMMI / JOURNALIST / JASMINE / LOLA / JOJO / CARA / BEAU / SUZ / NINA / KATHRYN / VIDA.

SOFIA / DANIEL / MUM / BOYS / AGATHA / CRAIG / PK 1 / DELILAH / LEON / FRAN / JOY / PATTY / CLEM.

DARBY / CARL / RUPERT / FINN / OFFICIAL / PK 2 / MARC / AUGIE / AIDEN / RAMI / MORRIE / KIT / SASHI / ARCHIE.

NOTE ON DOUBLING

This is a play for three performers, with doubling as above.

NOTE ON TEXT

Lines in italics denote dialogue between characters.

/ marks the point of interruption in a sentence.

SETTING

Here, not far from now.

This play went to press before the end of rehearsals and may differ from the play as performed.

PROLOGUE

IMMI: Slap.
SOFIA: Bang.
DARBY: Kiss.
ALL: I feel the sting
IMMI: As my hand whips his face.
SOFIA: As the bullet slices my arm.
DARBY: As his lips press against mine.
SOFIA: It catches me off balance
DARBY: My knees wobble
IMMI: Fingers tingle
ALL: And my first instinct is to run.
DARBY: But then
IMMI: But then
SOFIA: I don't.
I don't run.
IMMI: I stare at my hand, my hand that just slapped a peacekeeper.
DARBY: I press my lips against Daniel's and I can feel his stubble on my lip and I think: holy crap I'm actually doing it.
SOFIA: Heart pounding fast, pumping blood down my arm.
IMMI: I'm surprised at how much it stings.
SOFIA: So much blood.
DARBY: Rushing to my fingertips, to my cheeks.
IMMI: I thought I was stronger than that.
DARBY: My … you know.
SOFIA: Breathe.
DARBY: Breathe.
IMMI: Breathe.
SOFIA: You need to hide.
IMMI: Don't look away, look at him.
DARBY: Keep going, dickhead, enjoy it, you're kissing Daniel Koh!

Silence.

IMMI: I stare straight into the peacekeeper's eyes.
SOFIA: I look at the bullet wound on my arm.

DARBY: I feel Daniel Koh's stubbly moustache against my top lip and I know.
IMMI: I know, then, that nothing
DARBY: Nothing
SOFIA: Nothing is going to be the same as it was.

ONE

IMMI: Five to six and you can feel it, in the air, on your skin. Five to six and it's almost curfew.

Onto the street and bolt for the checkpoint, shortcut through the arcade, and something's up cos there's a crackle in the air. Streets feel angry and I do too, wound up tight, just waiting for the snap. Something's gunna go down tonight. Turn the corner to Checkpoint B: shit. Huge crowd. Friday night panic, people waving papers at the gate, desperate to get home before curfew. Like rats, I think. We're like rats being sent back to our holes for the night.

Three minutes.

Slip down the front, silent; no-one sees me. Dogs in muzzles, drones buzzing, peacekeepers everywhere. It gets like this, sometimes. Flash their dicks around, like to remind us who's in charge. Woman in front of me's piled up with bags and she wants them through, but the peacekeeper shakes his head, keeps shaking and she argues with him. Back and forth and the clock's counting down; come on, let her through, she has her papers and then slap.

Crowd falls silent.

He just fucking slapped her.

She scurries through and I do too. Head down, hand over papers, smile—bag check yes, ID card yes. The PK pats me down and I think:

You should be the one with papers, dick.

Six-oh-one. I'm through.

Head for home and shake it off, SLAP, the drones, the dogs, the crackle in the air and—

She stops. She looks up.

Where's the flag?

There, up there on our building roof—there used to be a flag up there. Our flag, flying high, hung by Gran but now: gone, replaced with theirs.

My hand twitches.

Look down along the fence line. Closing us in more 'n' more each day. Checkpoint to the north, to the south, the east, the west. Surrounded. Cameras, watching. PKs on the street. This is what they've done to us. Hunted us into a corner, told us we don't exist.

My hand twitches and I realise, then.

Yeah.

Yeah something is gunna go down tonight.

And I'm gunna be the one to start it.

Look up and spot one, stationed up ahead.

OI. Yeah you peacekeeper fuck. *GET OFF MY STREET.*

Barely turns his head he does and that's enough for me, and then I'm run, run back toward him, fast and faster, getting speed, getting fire:

I said Get. Off. My. Street.

Nothing.

Don't ignore me, pig.

His head snaps. Ooh. Nibble nibble. My hand twitches again. *When are you gunna take your tanks and fuck OFF, these streets are ours. Ours before you came and ours when we get you gone. So GET OUT. GET OUT GET OUT GET OUT* and as my voice grows loud I start to see:

People, watching.

High up in windows, all around.

See curtains open, phones out filming.

Filming me.

She looks at her hand.

My cousin's pain, my hand. My brother's pain my hand. My mother's pain, my grandmother's pain, every one of us that they've forced into this cage, their pain in my hand, their rage in my hand and I know what I have to do:

SLAP.

Silence.

Owww.

I feel the sting and his head turns,

slowly,

toward me.

I can't believe I just did that.

Step back, back away from the peacekeeper, away from the bomb I've just dropped, and all I can feel is the sting of slap, slap, slap

SOFIA: Bang

IMMI: Slap

SOFIA: Bang

IMMI: Slap

SOFIA: Bang my foot against the desk.

Two-nineteen.

Reeks in here. Like someone farted, deodorant, nasty socks.

Two-nineteen and we're still on Famous Speeches by Shakespeare, Cassius to Brutus, Hamlet, Richard, Henry, 'Sir, has someone in the English department cross-checked this list for a character without a dick?'

Don't say that, obviously. Don't say anything. Goff's staring at us in silence, waiting for an answer to a question no-one even remembers. *This is shit* Kevin shouts. I feel sorry for Goff but Kevin's right, this is shit.

Two-nineteen.

Phone dings in my pocket, shit: Jye. 'Get out.' Type back: 'I wish bitch I'm in English and I think my brain is leaking out my ears, RIP me.'

And then the fire alarm goes off. Laughing, jeers, Kevin again: *Sir you know the school has to pay for the fire trucks if it's a false alarm*. Press send.

Wait for the alarm to stop.

Except it doesn't. Goff stands, frowns.

Two-twenty.

People say bad shit happens in slow motion. That you tune in to tiny details.

Two-twenty and the door clicks and we all turn, because, duh, we hear the door click, and he's there, and he's holding this gun, and it sprays into the room, a wave of dull pops, and Rebecca next to me she drops out of the air, and then me too, I'm on the ground. I've been shot. I know that I've been shot and I look at the clock.

Still two-twenty. Lie on the ground and listen as he turns, closes the door, walks away, up the hall, bang, bang, bang

DARBY: *Kiss*

SOFIA: Bang

DARBY: *Kiss*

SOFIA: Bang

DARBY*: Kiss, Jasmine, I'm going to KISS Daniel Koh.*

JASMINE: *You?*

DARBY: *What does that mean?*

JASMINE: *Well Daniel Koh's, like, a hot rebel with a mullet and a nose ring and you ...*

DARBY*: Yes?*

JASMINE: *You're a weedy gay redhead from a deadshit town in the middle of nowhere.*

DARBY: *Correction, Jasmine: I'm a weedy gay redhead who's about to set a world record.*

There's just the three of us here: me, Jasmine and this student teacher who followed us here and keeps saying what we're doing is 'just so rad'—whatever, I look around for Daniel Koh.

JASMINE: *How long do you have to kiss for?*

DARBY: *Thirty-seven hours. You need to film it, get your phone.*

JASMINE: *Shouldn't we like, do it at your house?*

DARBY: *No, Jasmine, I'm not just going to invite him to make out in my HOUSE, that's weird, it needs to be somewhere, like, special.*

JASMINE: *Reckon he knows you're in love with him?*

DARBY: *I'm not in love with him Jasmine shut up he's here.*

Hi.

DANIEL: *Hi.*

DARBY: *Hi.*

DANIEL: *You look cute.*

DARBY: Oh my god.

Thanks. I like your ... shoes.

DANIEL: ... *Thanks. They're just school shoes.*

DARBY: Good one, Darby.

So we just need to pick somewhere to actually. Do it.

DANIEL: *Why not here?*

DARBY*: Here?*

JASMINE: *In the Woolworths car park?*

DANIEL: *Why not? Make a splash.*

JASMINE: *I—*

DARBY*: Yes. Okay. Great idea. Tweet it Jasmine. We're doing it here. Ready?*

DANIEL: *Ready.*

DANIEL *nods.*

JASMINE *holds up her phone and speaks into the camera.*

JASMINE: *Hi. I'm Jasmine. It's four o'clock on Friday the twelfth of April, give or take a few seconds, and as you can see, here we are in the beautiful Woolworths car p—*

DARBY: *Jasmine, just say the thing.*

JASMINE: *Sorry, god, okay. This is the official recording of Darby and Daniel's world record attempt for the longest kiss. I hope I have enough battery. Ready?*

DARBY: Daniel looks at me. I want to spew. I can't believe this is actually happening, like actually really—

JASMINE: *Kiss!*

DARBY: He leans in and he is so hot and Oh god, Darby Kang, you're in trouble now.

JASMINE: *Kiss, kiss.*

DARBY: And we do.
We …
Kiss.

SOFIA: Bang.

IMMI: Slap.

Silence.

I stare into the peacekeeper's eyes as I back away from him.

SOFIA: Heart pounding fast, pumping blood down my arm.

DARBY: I feel Daniel Koh's stubbly moustache against my top lip and I know.

SOFIA: I know.

IMMI: I know, then, that nothing
DARBY: Nothing
SOFIA: Nothing is going to be the same as it was.

TWO

IMMI: Mum whips round, eyes huge as she screams:
MUM: *What the hell was that Immi?*
IMMI: Not anger in her voice but something else—
MUM: *Do you have any idea what you've done?*
IMMI: Fear. She's afraid.
MUM: *You think they're just going to let you get away with that?*
IMMI: *They don't control me—*
MUM: *Yes they do. They control all of us, okay?*
IMMI: *That was Gran's flag, and this is OUR home.*
MUM: *You sound just like her.*
IMMI: *I'm glad someone does.*
MUM: *This is their home, Immi, ever since those tanks rolled in and they said 'this is ours now'.*
IMMI: *But—*
MUM: *They can do whatever they want to us, understand? You've just given them permission to do anything they want.*
IMMI: Kick round my room, heart racing. Try and focus on something, anything else: sound of the news upstairs, dogs barking outside. Close my eyes but SLAP. Still feel the hot sting of skin on skin. And then the door: my brother with dinner
RUPERT: *Were you seriously wearing a Minnie Mouse T-shirt when you slapped a peacekeeper?*
IMMI: *It's ironic, dickhead.*
RUPERT: *Mum's losing her shit y'know. Reckons they're gunna raid us cos of you.*
IMMI: *Yeah, well.*
RUPERT: *You're so angry these days*
IMMI: *Fucken duh, Rupert. Aren't you?*
RUPERT: *Being angry's not gunna get you anywhere you know. It's just gunna make it harder for the rest of us.*
Here's some beans. I ate the cheese.

IMMI: And then he's gone.

And the room feels empty.

And I'm scared, suddenly.

My hand hurts and I miss Gran.

Think it's been hours, but my phone says ten-thirty.

Don't know what to do. Don't know why I did it. Don't know why I thought anyone would give a shit. We're rats. And the world hates rats. The world can't even point to us on a map.

I eat cold beans and I paint my toes and the walls close in, slowly, slow, until I close my eyes and sleep.

—

SOFIA: Blink into the dark.

In the cupboard next to the stairs, me and this Year Eight Carl. He can't stop talking.

CARL: *You alright? You're bleeding.*

SOFIA: Look at the graze on my arm, black with blood. I can't tell if it hurts, can't tell if it's still bleeding or—

CARL: *It's okay, you don't have to talk.*

SOFIA: We're hidden, by shelves of cricket bats and footballs, those weird CPR training dolls. Rows of plastic corpses, waiting for breath to be pumped into them.

CARL: *Resusci Anne. Those dolls, that's what they're called. They modelled the face on a woman they found drowned in the River Seine in 1885. That's why she looks so dead. Cos she was. Is.*

SOFIA: How does he know that?

CARL: *You have to use your whole upper body weight when you're doing CPR, and press hard but not so hard that you break a rib, that's a common misconception that you're meant to break a rib, you're not.*

Sorry.

Are you okay?

SOFIA: He shivers.

CARL: *My T-shirt's out there. We were in the middle of a game when ...*

Beat.

SOFIA: It's quiet.

The bangs have stopped.

This room must back on to the canteen because I can hear the hum of the fridges. And as Carl starts telling me about how you score in cricket, I suddenly think: Why doesn't this feel more weird?

CARL: *Do you reckon it's over?*

SOFIA: Six years of safety training demonstrations, six years of get under your chairs kids, learn how to hide, kids, how to lock doors behind you—

CARL: *It must be over, right?*

SOFIA: They teach us these things in case it happens, and then it fucking happens, a self-fulfilling prophecy.

CARL: *It must be over.*

SOFIA: No, I want to say, I don't think it is.

—

DARBY: There's this, like, energy, pulsing through us, through Daniel Koh and me and We Are Connected. Like obviously yes at the mouth but also, our souls, which sounds dramatic but actually it's just … hot.

JASMINE: *Darby it's been like two hours, and there's seven people here. Didn't you put up flyers or something?*

DARBY: That's when when I hear it, underneath the whine in Jasmine's voice: a car, engine revving on the other side of the car park.

JASMINE: *Darbs do you reckon I can go get hot chips and come back?*

DARBY: Hear the crunch of tyres on gravel and then … acceleration.

JASMINE: *What's that noise?*

DARBY: Coming toward us.

JASMINE: *Can you hear that?*

DARBY: Rumble of the engine and then that sound that jocks make when they want you to know they're descended from Neanderthal man.

BOYS: *NGYYEAHH.*

JASMINE: *Shit!*

DARBY: Louder, closer, the car comes straight toward us.

BOYS: *NNNGGGGYEAAAAAAHHHH.*

DARBY: And as it screeches past, something hits me and Daniel Koh in the side of the head.

BOYS: *FAGGOTS.*

DARBY: Time freezes.

JASMINE: *What the hell?*

DARBY: My face stings, head throbs.

JASMINE: *ARSEHOLES.*

DARBY: It's a brick or, a book, a phone?

JASMINE: *Are you okay?*

DARBY: Something wet runs down our faces. Blood. No, sweeter than that, piss! Running down our faces and into our mouths, sweet and sticky, like—

JASMINE: *Darby?*

DARBY: Grape. It's not piss, it's—

JASMINE: *Oh my god. Someone just threw a fucking Slurpee at them.*

DARBY: And then it all rushes at me: pain, fear, everything that's ever been thrown at me. I can feel Daniel Koh try to pull away, but I grab hold of him, press my body into his and he …

He stops pulling away.

JASMINE: *We should call the cops, right? Shouldn't we call the cops?*

DARBY: Maybe I don't stop kissing him because I don't want anyone to see the stinging red of my cheeks.

JASMINE: *Those arseholes.*

DARBY: Maybe because I don't want to give up a world record attempt.

JASMINE: *I have it all on film.*

DARBY: Maybe I just really like kissing Daniel Koh.

JASMINE: *I got their number plate and everything.*

DARBY: I hold him tight and all I can taste is grape and … salt. Shit, I'm—crying. Great, now I'm the weedy gay readhead who cried.

JASMINE: *Fuck.*

It's back.

The car, it's back.

DARBY: Sounds of screeching as the car chucks a ewie and comes straight back toward us

BOYS: *NNNGGGGYEAAAAAAHHHH*

DARBY: What now, what are they going to do to us now? The brakes screech and the car … stops.

Open my eyes.

Without saying a word, the seven people who are there, they've moved. They've surrounded us, in a circle, holding hands, like … armour.

JASMINE: *We've got you*
DARBY: They say, as me and Daniel Koh keep kissing.
JASMINE: *Don't worry. We've got you. We've got you.*

THREE

SOFIA: 'We've got you', the cops whisper as they hustle us out, passing us down the senior corridor, then shouting:
COP: *Keep down, run! Leave everything behind!*
SOFIA: Single file through eerie silence, empty rooms, past the locker someone's pushed up against a door and this still doesn't feel weird.
CARL: *Sofia. This way.*
SOFIA: Out front of the school and there's people crying: kids, teachers and then parents behind barriers, reporters, cameras, helicopters, why doesn't this feel weird? It's like I've seen it before, seen a girl like me running scared from a building just like that.
CARL: *Are you okay?*
SOFIA: Cameras flashing. Squint into the sun, that plastic doll's face burned into my retinas. I'm frozen and the world spins.

Nothing's changed.

I got shot. Rebecca's blood is on my shoes, and that's when I hear a journalist, there, saying something into a camera:
JOURNALIST: *Leaders across the political divide have offered their thoughts and prayers to the victims.*
SOFIA: Suddenly the pain in my arm is searing hot and I wanna scream.

I turn and walk straight toward a camera, and it's like they know, they know that I'm coming for them, and they must be waiting for me because as I step over the barrier a microphone in my face, bang:

Speak. Speak.

She looks down the barrel of the camera.

We don't want your thoughts and prayers. Alright? Why do you keep letting this happen? The last time this happened you said the same thing and Nothing. Changed. Every time you offer your thoughts and prayers, one of us dies.

She steps closer to the camera.

So do something. Do. Something.

And remember this face. Because I'm coming for your thoughts and prayers. And I'm really pissed off.

—

IMMI: Sky's red, apocalyptic.

Stillness all round.

Street empty.

Windows empty.

No movement, nowhere.

I have this feeling that the world used to be this quiet, once, this quiet and still, and then—a rumble. Like an earthquake, maybe, but deeper than that; right under me, under the building, in the ground, in the middle of the earth. Look out my bedroom window, down to the intersection and—framed under streetlight:

Gran.

Except it can't be Gran, we buried her two years ago, but then I see that twinkle in her eye, gummy toothless grin. *Gran!* Her smile fades, lips form into words. *What? Grandma I can't hear you?* She says it again, but I can't hear her, can't hear through the glass, *Gran? Gran! Speak up!* And I press my hand against the window, ow, it's hot, burning, my hand it's burning and—

—

DARBY: Open my eyes still sticky with grape. I must be dreaming because when Daniel Koh opens his eyes it's like he's staring right at me. Right, like, into me?

It's really intense looking directly at someone while you're making out with them, like once you get past the weird bit you have this really full-on connection that I think … actually, now that it's happening, it might mean that Daniel Koh and I, we're falling in—

JASMINE: *You're a spineless turd, Evan Simpson! Shit.*

DARBY: Way to kill a moment, Jasmine.

JASMINE: *Darby you have to look at this. Turn around.*

DARBY: Okay it's actually quite difficult to turn around when you're attached to someone at the mouth—

JASMINE: *Just spin, c'mon.*

DARBY: Daniel Koh's eyes sparkle and that's how I know he'd be smiling, if he could. I try and sparkle my eyes back and then, pressed together at the lips we … spin, like some sort of life-sized super-gay two-man mirror-ball. Surrounding us, arms linked, there's Jasmine and Kip and Fahad and the student teacher and—did Evan leave?!

JASMINE: *Evan LEFT! He said he was going to 'get in trouble' if he missed dinner. Can you believe that?*

DARBY: Actually I sort of can because instead of romantic this whole thing is starting to feel kind of pathetic.

JASMINE: *What if those boys come back?*

DARBY: Like who's going to fall in love covered in frozen syrup in a car park?

JASMINE: *What if they come back and bring like, cricket bats or something?*

What if they come and do actual violence?

DARBY: I want to tell her that throwing a missile at someone's head is actual violence but …

It's really dark in this car park.

What if she's right?

I know Daniel Koh's thinking it too.

JASMINE: *We need backup.*

DARBY: Then she disappears from my line of vision, can't see her but can hear her voice:

JASMINE: *If there's anyone watching out there, consider this an S.O.S. Help us.*

DARBY: Jasmine what do you mean 'anyone watching out there'? Who are you talking to?

JASMINE: *Get in your cars and get down here.*

DARBY: Jasmine are you doing a Live? You're meant to be recording.

JASMINE: *Backup required.*

DARBY: No, no backup required, focus!

JASMINE: *These boys need our protection. This isn't just about a world record anymore—*

DARBY: Yes it is, Jasmine, FOCUS.

JASMINE: *This is about the fundamental right for two relatively cute boys to be outside, in the world, doing their thing without someone throwing a Slurpee at them.*

Use the hashtag RainbowRing. No, that sounds gross. RainbowArmy. Help us. Please. We need you.

FOUR

SOFIA: Open my eyes and lurch from sleep, suddenly awake. For a second I don't know where I am, what's happened, why my arm is bandaged, my head pounding and—

IMMI: —I'm out, early, pacing the perimeter, past checkpoints, past tradies waiting for curfew to break. Some bloke yells out at me, *DICKHEAD* I yell back, *SQUEAK SQUEAK.* I keep—

DARBY: —going but far out no-one tells you how tired your tongue gets when you've been making out with someone for ten hours, and not just my tongue but my whole body, it's like I've been running a marathon, legs aching, eyes—

SOFIA: —open and stare at the ceiling. The last twenty-four hours come back to me: Jye's message ding, the door clicking open and then the microphone: bang.

IMMI: When I walk these streets they're mine, the footprints mine, the imprint I make mine, and even when they take everything else, they can't take—

DARBY: —that creeping feeling that maybe this whole thing was stupid, stupid and dangerous, I just wanted him to fall in love with me—

IMMI: —but pacing circles around the fence line's exactly what a rat does and I—

SOFIA: —roll over on my side and wince in pain and I—

DARBY: —feel the tired weight of Daniel Koh leaning against me and I—

IMMI: —keep getting weird looks from random people so I put my hood up and—

DARBY: —lean into him, breathe, and I am—

ALL: Hit.

SOFIA: By this overwhelming feeling.

ALL: I'm so

IMMI: So

DARBY: So

ALL: … tired.

IMMI: Tired of pushing up and being pushed back down, being trapped, being watched all the time.

DARBY: Of always and forever waiting for something to hit me in the side of the head, a fist, a brick, a spit soaked sausage roll.

SOFIA: Tired of running this soundtrack of horrors over and over in my head.

ALL: I want to give up.

SOFIA: Go back to sleep.

DARBY: Stuff the record and go home.

IMMI: Stop walking, stop everything.

ALL: No-one tells you it's going to be this hard.

Silence.

DARBY: But then

IMMI: But then

SOFIA: But then I hear my phone vibrating, under my pillow.

IMMI: I see something, tagged on the fence.

DARBY: I hear a car, driving across the car park.

SOFIA: Grab it and the screen, it's full of notifications.

IMMI: Move closer and touch the tag, still wet.

DARBY: The car stops and parks, engine off.

IMMI: It's ears. Mouse ears, with whiskers and—

SOFIA: Messages, tags, comments, emails.

DARBY: Car door opens, closes.

IMMI: A mouse drawn in thick black texta, right there on the brick.

SOFIA: There's a newspaper article with a picture of me, microphone in hand.

IMMI: I look down at my T-shirt

ALL: And the first thing I think is:

DARBY: The Live.

SOFIA: The interview.

IMMI: The video.

ALL: It's out.

SOFIA: *'Teen Goes Wild on Guns'*

IMMI: Words next to the ears: 'SQUEAK SQUEAK'.

DARBY: Standing next to the car: this normal looking woman, holding her handbag.

SOFIA: Open my bedroom curtains and I'm blinded by the flash of cameras all over my front lawn
IMMI: I suddenly feel like the whole world is looking at me, right at me.
SOFIA: News crews and journalists spilling onto the footpath.
DARBY: *I saw your message*, says the woman.
SOFIA: What the hell, shut the curtains, breathe.
DARBY: *I'm here to help, I want to join your Rainbow Army thing.*
IMMI: I'm the mouse. I'm the mouse. I'm the fucking mouse!

FIVE

IMMI: Turn and run, back on to the street, head for home.
IMMI/AGATHA/FINN: Stop.
FINN: Whoa, is that—
AGATHA: See her, looking at something.
IMMI: Tagged on a power pole: mouse. Mouse on the side of a truck, a billboard. What's going on?
FINN: Follow her across the street
AGATHA: Pounding steps, one, two, then skip
IMMI: Skip over trash on the road
AGATHA: I know it's her, the girl next door
AGATHA/FINN: I watched the video this morning
FINN: Recognise her T-shirt
AGATHA: And then the boy from the fruit shop runs up to her
FINN: I run up to her and she
IMMI/AGATHA/FINN: Stops.
FINN: *Are you—*
IMMI: *What?*
FINN: She looks at me weirdly.
IMMI: He looks at me weirdly.
AGATHA: They look at each other weirdly. Can't hear what they're saying but—
FINN: *You're the mouse.*
Right?
AGATHA: He points at her T-shirt.
FINN: *I saw you on the internet this morning.*
You got that PK good.

My dad reckons you're gunna start a revolution.

AGATHA: She doesn't move at all.

FINN: *Squeak squeak.*

AGATHA: And then she turns

FINN: Runs across the road

AGATHA: And into our building

IMMI: Up the stairs, two at a time, one storey, two, and open the door to our apartment.

AGATHA: Press my ear to the wall:

IMMI: *Mum have you seen online? Have you seen?*

AGATHA: Footsteps down her corridor, then silence.

Silence.

IMMI: Four peacekeepers at the kitchen table, and then a fifth person, in a suit.

An official.

OFFICIAL: *We have a little problem, you see.*
We're a peaceful society.
And you have broken that peace.

IMMI: Mum's eyes are huge and my heart pounds in my chest.

OFFICIAL: *You need to apologise. To the peacekeeper you attacked. Say sorry. Say you were wrong to do what you did. Say he was protecting you. That he was keeping the peace, and you were the one who broke it.*

IMMI: He sneers like he's up himself then leans in close:

OFFICIAL: *Because if you don't—do you know the punishment for violently assaulting a peacekeeper?*

IMMI: And I can smell it on him, a smell I know all too well because I smell it all round me, all the time.

Fear.
He knows. He knows it's on the streets and now this man
is scared
of me.

And it comes to me, then, like a vision: Gran under streetlight, her words crystal in my head: 'Keep going, little mouse.'

OFFICIAL: *This is a one time offer.*

IMMI: And I know what I have to do.

Okay. Yes. I want to apologise to the man I slapped.

OFFICIAL: *Wonderf—*

IMMI: *I want you to tell him that I'm sorry he got in my way. And not just him, I'm sorry to my family, and my friends, to every one of us who you grind down with your bullshit, every one of us that has to leave work early or goes to a segregated school or who can't marry who they want, can't vote, I'm sorry to them that it's taken me this long to stand up and say out loud Fuck You. I'm sorry that it's taken me this long to get here, and I'm sorry I had to slap someone to make it happen, but I did, and I'm here now. So: Fuck You.*

This 'little problem' isn't going anywhere.

Silence.

AGATHA: Shit.

OFFICIAL: She steps forward, looks me right in the eye.

IMMI: *And you know what they say, right? Where there's one mouse, there's many.*

AGATHA: Then shouts, screams; open my door and they're on the stairs, her in handcuffs—

IMMI: *MY NAME IS IMMI MARCUS.*

OFFICIAL: *Get back inside.*

IMMI: *MY NAME IS IMMI MARCUS AND I AM SIXTEEN YEARS OLD.*

AGATHA: Her brother filming, people in the stairwell, filming.

OFFICIAL: *Stop filming!*

AGATHA: And from a place I didn't think I had left in me, I scream back: *Don't stop filming, don't stop filming!*

—

DARBY: Don't stop filming! Jasmine! They need to see continuous footage else it's not a valid entry, I told you that.

JASMINE: *Darby, can you hear me in there?*

DARBY: I'm not in a coma.

JASMINE: *If you can hear me, blink once. I really think you should look at this, look!*

DARBY: Flick my eyes side to side: maybe twenty or thirty people standing around us, holding hands—

JASMINE: *It's working, Darbs. People are coming! Real people!*

CRAIG: *Sorry who's the organiser of ... whatever this is?*

JASMINE: *That'd be me.*

DARBY: Actually it's me, Jasmine.

CRAIG: *Craig, I'm the customer service manager on duty.*

JASMINE: *Great to have you on board, jump in anywhere you like.*

CRAIG: *No, I'm not joining, I need you to move.*

DARBY: Silence from Jasmine. Never a good sign.

JASMINE: *Sorry?*

CRAIG: *Move, you need to move. Now. You're blocking access to the trolleys.*

JASMINE: *Can't everyone just go that way instead?*

CRAIG: *No.*

JASMINE: *Why?*

CRAIG: *Because this is the pathway to the trolleys.*

DARBY: Oh boy.

JASMINE: *Oh. Oh this is the pathway to the trolleys, is it, Craig?*

DARBY: Jasmine, take a deep breath—

JASMINE: *In case you haven't noticed, we're using this area right now.*

CRAIG: *Listen, lady—*

DARBY: Don't call her lady.

JASMINE: *Don't call me lady, my name is Jasmine.*

CRAIG: *Okay Jasmine, this is private land. What are you even protesting?*

JASMINE: *This isn't a protest, Craig, this is the first line of defense.*

DARBY: Actually it's a world record attempt.

JASMINE: *Because last night someone threw a sour grape Slurpee at my best friend here and his crush who he has been wanting to kiss for a very long time and I'm pretty sure they're in love now—*

DARBY: Shit, Jasmine.

JASMINE: *So we decided they need protection, Craig, from your customers.*

CRAIG: *Oh.*

JASMINE: *You're not going to let two teenage boys who are just trying to set a world record remain unprotected from your violent customers, are you Craig?*

CRAIG: *No.*

JASMINE: *Correct. So let's try that again, shall we—you repeat after me, Craig: this isn't the pathway to the trolleys.*

CRAIG: *This isn't the pathway to the trolleys.*

JASMINE: *This is the pathway to progress.*

Beat.

DARBY: She's an absolute nightmare most of the time but god I love you Jasmine.

CRAIG: *Can you just shift the pathway to progress half a metre that way so cars can get through?*

JASMINE: *No.*

CRAIG: *Okay.*

JASMINE: *Craig?*

CRAIG: … *Yes Jasmine.*

JASMINE: *You should join us.*

DARBY: As a chorus of cheers go up from the crowd around us, Jasmine whispers

JASMINE: *I don't care what they try and make us do, Darby, you are gunna get this record.*

Don't forget to breathe.

—

SOFIA: 'Don't forget to breathe up there', I whisper to my reflection as I wash my hands.

I stop.

Run my fingers through the fresh bristles on my head and for the first time in my life I feel like … like I'm looking at a reflection of me.

LOLA: *Sofia? You in there?*

SOFIA/AUGIE: Lola.

AUGIE: I think that's her name, I taught her in Year Seven maybe? She knocks on the door again.

LOLA: I knock again: *You okay in there?*

SOFIA: *Coming,* I say.

AUGIE: And when Sofia opens the door, she has this look on her face—

LOLA: *Holy shitballs.*

SOFIA: *I did it last night, is it—bad?*

AUGIE: She's shaved her head, and Lola reaches out, touches it.

LOLA: *You look—*

AUGIE: She looks—

SOFIA: *I look like an old man, don't I?*

LOLA: *No, dude.*

AUGIE: She looks like she's ready for battle.

LOLA: *It's sick.*

You ready?

AUGIE: Lola grabs Sofia's hand and they turn, head up the senior corridor, and I grab my folder for period eight and follow them, out the staffroom toward the gym, toward the memorial.

SOFIA: Feels like everyone's watching. *Is everyone looking at me?*

LOLA: *Duh, Sof, you got shot, yelled at the TV and then shaved your head, what do you want them to do?*

AUGIE: Students pour into the corridor around us, families, teachers, and the girls get lost up ahead.

SOFIA: Past the senior common room

LOLA: The arts billboard

AUGIE: Everyone following her like some kind of Year Ten Pied Piper.

Squish onto the basketball court and watch as the two friends wave.

SOFIA: Lola waves to me, whispers

LOLA: *You can do this. I love you,* and then she's gone

AUGIE: Whisked away behind the temporary stage maintenance have built

SOFIA: Mrs Chapman talks me through the rundown

AUGIE: Rita hands me a program

LOLA: Miss Chu sends me down the front to watch

AUGIE: Brian tells a Year Eight to get down off the basketball ring but actually there's no room so she stays up there

LOLA: Speakers start and end

SOFIA: I'm next, and even though normally I'd be shaking and nervous …

for some reason,

I'm not.

LOLA: She steps onto the stage.

AUGIE: The whole gym breathes in.

SOFIA: I breathe at the microphone.

LOLA: We wait.

AUGIE: The room is full, of sadness, grief, anger, but as she stands in front of us …

LOLA: You can hear a pin drop.

AUGIE: There's something else.

Hope.

SOFIA: *I want to tell you about my friends. About my friends who died. They were waiting. Like us. For the bell to ring. For English to finish. For replies to their texts. Waiting to see if they got into the musical, waiting for the weekend.*

They were just like us. Waiting to be a casualty in another school shooting.

AUGIE: She says all the things we've heard before, but in her mouth, they sound different.

LOLA: I look back, at everyone crammed into the gym, the way they're listening to her, and … I realise that even though today isn't about her—it kind of is.

SOFIA: *I don't want to spend the rest of my school years waiting to be shot. Training to be shot. It's a fact that people walk into schools with guns and shoot teenagers. But the only way anything changes is if people change it. I'm not talking to the teachers, or the parents up the back, or any adults watching this at home. I'm talking to you. You in front me right now. The only way anything changes is if you change it. Do something. Do something. Do. Something.*

SIX

PK 2: *You see what they did to the billboard out front?*

PK 1: *Third time this week.*

Why's she pacing like that?

PK 2: *Dunno. She's been doing it since they brought her in.*

PK 1: *She's so ... small. Isn't she? The way they talked about her in the papers it's like she was—*

PK 2: *What?*

PK 1: *Well—she's a kid. A skinny kid.*

PK 2: *A skinny kid who picked a fight.*

You know her grandma's the reason they put in the checkpoints, right? Started the first resistance. Whole family are toxic agitators. It's in her blood.

PK 1: *Do you reckon she knows?*

PK 2: *That she's on the front page of every newspaper in the world?*
PK 1: *That they're calling her a hero.*
PK 2: *Course she bloody knows.*
JOJO: My phone goes, on my bed.
PK 2: *She planned the whole thing.*
JOJO: I reach over and grab it, hold it in front of my face.
RAMI: I've been added to a new thread—MARCH.
JOJO: MARCH? In capitals, two lightning bolts either side.
RAMI: Open, no messages yet but a hundred and twelve people in the chat.
JOJO: Kids from school but mostly numbers I don't recognise. 'Hey what's this?'
RAMI: 'Who started this?'
JOJO: People sending question marks, the eyeglass
RAMI: An eggplant, obviously.
JOJO: And then a one line message, from her.
RAMI: From Sofia:
JOJO/RAMI: 'We need to do something.'
JOJO: No one replies, then again from her:
RAMI: 'We can't just go back to our lives like nothing changed.'
JOJO: 'On Friday afternoon, at two-nineteen, one week since the shooting, we're walking out of our classrooms.'
RAMI: 'We're marching on Parliament.'
I sit up properly.
JOJO: 'We have to do something. People have to know how angry we are.'

Beat.

RAMI: 'Who's *we*'?
JOJO: No one answers for a second, then Sofia replies:
RAMI: 'Everyone.
Who's in?'
JOJO: Me, I write.
RAMI: Me.
JOJO: And as the flood of me's start pouring in—
RAMI: 'me',
JOJO: 'me',

RAMI: 'me'

JOJO: —more people get added to the thread, from our school, other schools, then interstate, across the country.

RAMI: Everyone planning, organising.

JOJO: Sub-committees start:

RAMI: someone's dad's got a speaker,

JOJO: a truck we can use to move things,

RAMI: a workshop for banner-making.

JOJO: 'Tell everyone' the messages say.

RAMI: 'Tell everyone, bring everyone.'

DANIEL: Open my eyes and there he is.

RAMI: 'Spread the word.'

DANIEL: Darby Kang, a whisp of hair fallen across his forehead.

JASMINE: *Hi boys, how you going in there?*

DANIEL: God he's cute.

JASMINE: *There's nearly two hundred people out here, can you believe that?*

DANIEL: I shuffle cos my leg's cramping and my mouth is basically a wound.

JASMINE: *About ten of them are just trying to get to the trolleys but—*

DANIEL: I search for Darby's hand, squeeze, and he squeezes back.

JASMINE: *Emma spoke to Rashida who spoke to someone who said they drove SIX HOURS to get here.*

DANIEL: If I flick my eyes I can see signs, banners, and oh god there's a ukulele.

JASMINE: *Why does someone always bring a ukulele?*

DANIEL: Ignore all that, and focus on the fact that I, Daniel Koh, am kissing Darby Kang, the cutest boy in school.

JASMINE: *Unfortunately there is a tiny little issue.*

DANIEL: What?

JASMINE: *Well, firstly, there's quite a few news crews around which is blocking the street, and well the cops aren't THAT happy that we're causing a Category 2 Traffic Disturbance. Small fine, don't worry—*

DANIEL: Get to the point Jasmine.

JASMINE: *But the real problem is that, well.*

Someone reported the stream. For 'violating community standards'.

DANIEL: I feel Darby's body tense in my hands.

JASMINE: *It's been flagged as 'under review'.*

DANIEL: What does that mean, what does—

JASMINE: *They've taken it down.*

Beat.

DANIEL: Darby slumps.
Under my hands.
I have to literally hold him up else he's going to fall over.

JASMINE: *I'm really sorry.*

DANIEL: He looks at me sadly and for the second time today tears dribble into our mouths.

JASMINE: *It's over.*

DANIEL: He tries to pull away, to give up, but—
But I don't let him. I grab hold of him. I press my body into his.
I love you Darby Kang, and I said I was going to kiss you for thirty-seven hours and record or no record,

MARC: *Hi!*

DANIEL: that is exactly what I'm going to do.

MARC: *I'm Marc, I'm um, volunteering for the march tomorrow?*

DELILAH: *Everyone here is volunteering for the march tomorrow Marc.*

MARC: *Oh—*

DELILAH: *You don't go here right?*

MARC: *No, I go to—*

DELILAH: *Cool, but actually we're on a deadline so: I've got you on badges, I'm Delilah, nice to meet you.*

MARC: *I'm Marc—*

DELILAH: *You said that already. How did you hear about us?*

MARC: *My friend posted something on—*

DELILAH: *Your options are: 'word of mouth' or 'internet'.*

MARC: *Uh, internet? There's a lot of people here.*

DELILAH: *Yeah, we WERE just in the library and then all these people kept showing up so we took over the Year 12 common room as well, and then the gym and the outdoor basketball courts and then the business next door loaned us their offices, and now we're working on a third location AND a fourth, and satellites in every state in the country. Team Badge. This is Marc.*

MARC: *Hi, I'm Marc—*

DELILAH: *I said that already. Pick a picture, there's three: gun, target, bullet, then put it in that cradle thing and punch down.*

MARC: *Punch—*

DELILAH: *Down, yes. Then flip, pin, press, and you're done. Except we need like a million. But Marc?*

MARC: *Yes?*

DELILAH: *Literally a million. Like literally literally not figuratively literally.*

MARC: *You're expecting a million people?*

DELILAH: *Well as far as I can see, there's no reason every single teenager in the country shouldn't be marching, so actually I'm personally expecting something closer to seven million. People keep telling me I'm being 'unrealistically hopeful' but—*

CARA: *Why wouldn't I go?*

DELILAH: *I figure relentless hopefulness is all we've got, right?*

CARA: *It's not like anything's changed.*

AIDEN: *Seriously? You just said the stream got shut down.*

CARA: *Yeah but they haven't stopped kissing.*

AIDEN: *How do you know?*

CARA: *Because another stream popped up. Like fifty more actually. Everyone's started filming in protest and as more of them get shut down, more people keep arriving.*

AIDEN: *So now there's just fifty people filming two teenagers make out for no reason?*

CARA: *Actually there's like five hundred. And they're there to PROTECT them, Aiden. Obviously. And to prove that the power of their love is stronger than ...*

AIDEN: *What, a frozen drink?*

CARA: *Bigotry. And hate. Bigger than some dicks who throw missiles at people and some keyboard warrior who reckons they can shut the whole thing down because it 'offends' them.*

AIDEN: *Why do you have to make everything so political?*

CARA: *Because what if I want to kiss someone outside a Woolworths one day? Look at me. I am political, Aiden. I'm a whole lot of big dyke energy and I can't help it, I open my mouth and the word 'lesbian' falls out. I didn't make being me 'political', everyone else did. Everyone else made it so that when I walk down the street with my BDE it's a 'statement'.*

AIDEN: *Don't call it BDE.*

CARA: *They're not making a statement, they're just kissing. Can't they just fucking kiss?*

Beat.

AIDEN: *It's like three hours to get there. Dad'll flip if you take the good car.*

CARA: *I'm picking up the others in half an hour. I have room for one more.*

LEON: *But I'm only late because of the curfew!*

CARA: *So are you coming or not?*

LEON: *They don't even open the checkpoints till eight, shit.*

BEAU: Look over and the new guy's blown his top.

LEON: *Isn't it enough that you pay me half what you pay everyone else?*

BEAU/LEON: Shit.

BEAU: Kicks his toolbox, too hard and wet concrete sprays everywhere.

LEON: Foreman calls lunch.

BEAU/LEON: Sit, eat my sandwich.

BEAU: Watch him.

LEON: Clench and unclench my fist. Dick. We build their houses, pave their roads.

BEAU: Watch as he picks up a stick and digs it,

BEAU/LEON: deep into the wet concrete.

LEON: Heart pounding as I do it.

BEAU: Scrapes out one circle, another:

BEAU/LEON: Ears.

BEAU: A nose.

LEON: Whiskers.

Looks more like a cat, now, crap—

BEAU: *Oi.*

What're you doing?

LEON: *Just on break.*

Move my leg to cover the mouse but he sees. Idiot.

BEAU: *Intense, huh.*

LEON: *What is?*

BEAU: *Chucking a kid in a military prison.*

LEON: *Maybe she shouldn't have attacked that guy. He didn't do anything to her.*

BEAU: *Didn't he?*

There's a rumour that they're moving her to the courthouse, on Friday.

There's gunna be a protest.

You should come.

Beat.

LEON: *You being serious?*

BEAU: *You know what happens to people like her in places like that? No media, no public? They disappear. Except now the whole world's watching, and it's harder to made someone disappear when the whole world is watching. We just need to make sure they have something to watch.*

LEON: *Are you messing with me or—*

BEAU: *It doesn't have to be like this. Just cos it's been like this for so long doesn't mean it has to stay this way.*

Up to you man.

LEON: He hands me a scrap of paper.

BEAU: *That's the address.*

Friday. 4:30.

LEON: *You can't meet in public. Protest. They made that law, it's illegal.*

BEAU: *It's illegal to slap a peacekeeper too. But she still did it.*

Bring a stick.

SEVEN

MORRIE/SUZ/FRAN: Friday four-thirty.

People milling on the courthouse steps

MORRIE: but it's hard to tell who's here to protest and who's just here.

FRAN: Everyone's alone, finished work and

SUZ: staring at the ground, their phones.

MORRIE: Pull the scrap of paper out of my pocket and check the address. Right place.

FRAN: Wait, wait, / wait

SUZ: wait for something to happen,

ALL: and that's when I hear it.
MORRIE: This noise, coming from a group of people
FRAN: sitting on the steps, this
ALL: hissing.
FRAN: Look up. There's a woman, like me, alone.
MORRIE: Alone on the steps, and people are
SUZ: hissing at me.
MORRIE: She ignores them.
SUZ: I ignore them.
FRAN: Can't watch so I stare at the ground, don't want to attract attention but now they're
SUZ: talking about me too, I can hear them: catcalling, jeering,
MORRIE: about how she's dressed,
SUZ: how I smell,
FRAN: And then I see on her satchel, scratched in texta:
MORRIE: Two ears, whiskers.
FRAN: Two ears and whiskers. *Shit*
MORRIE: The hissing gets louder and
SUZ: everyone else around goes quiet,
FRAN: stops talking,
MORRIE: starts to walk away.
Everyone just leaves her, abandons her.
SUZ: I'm suddenly alone on the steps.
MORRIE: And then the group of hissers, they start to move. Toward her.
SUZ/FRAN: Oh god.
MORRIE: Six of them moving toward one woman alone, one against six.
FRAN: I put my headphones in and turn my music up, pretend I'm here for something else, but
MORRIE: her face,
FRAN: she looks so scared.
MORRIE: Before I know what I'm doing, I'm up.
FRAN: This old man stands up, across the square, he's on his feet
MORRIE: walking stick against my leg,
SUZ: hobbling, fast, toward me and I think: god another one, seven against one
FRAN: He winces.
MORRIE: We are all separate until something unites us.

FRAN: His eyes meet hers

MORRIE: and I nod

SUZ: and he stands by my side.

FRAN: He stands between her and the hissers.

MORRIE: Now it's two against six.

FRAN: And before I know what I'm doing I'm on my feet too, standing with them.

MORRIE: Three against six

FRAN: And then someone stands next to me

SUZ: Four.

MORRIE/SUZ/FRAN: We are all separate until something unites us.

MORRIE: *Squeak squeak.*

JOY/NINA/KIT: Tuesday two-nineteen.

The steps of the City Library are full, with people, noise, anger.

JOY: Watch from the café across the road: thousands of banners, kids in badges; watch this woman step off the tram and / onto the street

NINA: onto the street, god there's people everywhere, someone's definitely going to recognise me, a parent or a student.

JOY: She looks around

NINA: Try and hide behind these kids with a / huge banner

KIT: huge banner which weighs about a thousand kilos. Try to open it out properly but when I turn around I see—

NINA: *Kit!*

KIT: *Miss?*

Shit.

NINA: Sprung.

KIT: I should be in English right now.

NINA: I should be teaching him English right now.

JOY: They face each other, mouths agape.

KIT: *Sorry, Miss, I know that the note said we weren't allowed to skip class for this, but—*

JOY: Then the woman puts a finger to her lips, like:

NINA: *Shhhh.*

KIT: *You won't tell that we were here?*

JOY: Zips her lip.

KIT: Then she reaches out and pulls open the banner.

NINA/JOY: 'THIS ENDS WITH ME'

NINA: *Nice banner,*

KIT: she says to me.

NINA: *Hope you're right.*

JOY: And as she turns around and walks into the crowd, the banner folds closed again.

NINA: Except I think you're wrong, your banner's wrong.

JOY: He tries to keep the fabric aloft, spread it out but he struggles under its weight.

NINA: This won't end with you. You're too small, we all are.

JOY: And I can't watch this boy try and fail anymore so I ditch my coffee, push through the crowd and

KIT: This random lady grabs the other side and holds it up.

JOY: I want to tell him that this won't be the last time someone takes a gun into a school.

NINA/JOY: More people have to die.

KIT: It's heavy but I spent all night making it.

JOY: It's heavy but he doesn't seem to care, and as the speeches begin, the crowd they—

KATHRYN/PATTY/SASHI: Thirty-seven hours and the word goes around. Fifteen minutes till the boys have set the record.

KATHRYN: Sun's up as I get to the shop and the news wasn't wrong: whole town's been taken over by weird lookin / people everywhere

SASHI: people everywhere, literally, everywhere. I've never seen this many people in my life let alone in the middle of this deadshit town.

PATTY: Too many people to actually have eyes on Darby and Daniel, though, so I turn to the kid next to me and ask him *Can I've a boost?*

SASHI: *Sure*

PATTY: Hike up my dress and

KATHRYN: Shit, one of them drag queens is climbing up on top of the bus stop outside the bloody newsagent!

SASHI: There's feathers falling off her dress, raining down into my mouth and

KATHRYN: She looks like royalty or something, a queen lookin out at her kingdom.

SASHI: We have two cafés and an op-shop in this town, we do not have drag queens on bus stops.

PATTY: You are not in Kansas anymore doll.

SASHI: Then this guy in a Woolworths uniform shoves past us.

KATHRYN: A cry goes up and there's yelling, / everyone thinks he's being agro

PATTY: Everyone thinks he's being agro till we hear him calling out, shouting

ALL: *'Jasmine! The security cameras! We've got continuous footage on the security cameras!'*

KATHRYN: And suddenly the whole crowd goes nuts, cheering and laughing.

SASHI: I wonder if they have any idea, Darby and Daniel, I wonder if they even know what they've done.

PATTY: I try and take a photo but it's too big: the circle of people, fifty, a hundred rows deep maybe, spread out across the car park,

KATHRYN: spilling onto the road, blocking traffic, over footpaths and all the way down Main Street.

SASHI: A van handing out Solidarity Slurpees.

PATTY: People in costumes, waving flags.

SASHI: All holding hands. *Hey! Come over!*

KATHRYN: This boy he … waves at me. The boy that got feathers in his mouth.

SASHI: *Come join us.*

Beat. KATHRYN *joins* SASHI.

KATHRYN: I cross the road.
I stand at the back of the crowd and he grabs my arm.

SASHI: I link arms with her, the old lady from the newsagent.

KATHRYN: He smiles at me this … this huge big smile.

SASHI: She looks at me real weird.

KATHRYN: He looks so—happy.
And I think of all the time I spent being afraid of showing people in this little town who I really am.
I hold his hand tighter.
Thirty-seven hours.

JOY: Two-nineteen.

MORRIE: Four-thirty p.m.

Beat.

I look around the square,

KATHRYN: The car park

JOY: The steps of the library and there must be

MORRIE: Dozens of people

KATHRYN: Hundreds of people

JOY: Hundreds of thousands, maybe a million people across the city.

MORRIE: On the steps of the courthouse.

KATHRYN: Halfway to the edge of town.

MORRIE: The peacekeepers start to circle us.

KATHRYN: Old blokes linking arms with teenagers.

JOY: Families unfurl banners.

MORRIE: Everyone's hiding their faces with hankies.

JOY: Cops and ambos,

KATHRYN: parents with babies, tradies.

MORRIE: And together we start to shout her name, we carry her voice, *Her name is Immi Marcus.*

KATHRYN: And as word goes round that they've almost done it, just five more minutes and Darby and Daniel have set the record

JOY: The cheers and whistles begin, and we wait for Sofia to take the microphone, for her face to appear on the screens in front of us.

MORRIE: *Her name is Immi Marcus, her name is Immi Marcus.*

KATHRYN: We stamp our feet

JOY: Louder and louder

MORRIE: And it feels … improbable

KATHRYN: Impossible

MORRIE: That something so big could have been started by someone so small.

ALL: I have this feeling, then, as I look around

KATHRYN: That this,

JOY: this,

MORRIE: this is not just a moment in time.

JOY: Moments end.

KATHRYN: This

JOY: This

MORRIE: This is a movement.

A crescendo, and then silence.

EPILOGUE

From silence:

CLEM: The speeches are over.

Sofia's face is gone from the screen. Everyone's chatting as we wait for the march to begin. Wait for instructions, directions, for someone to lead us. Look down and see something—just there. A megaphone. *Does this belong to anyone?* I think that, I don't say it.

VIDA: It's four-forty-five and the square's full now. I tie my hanky tighter around my face. There's a crackle in the air, like something serious is gunna go down tonight. An unmarked van drives into the square and the crowd surges forward. It's her. We form a blockade, between her and the courthouse, and then a peacekeeper, right in my face shouting: '*YOU ARE COMMITING AN OFFENCE*' and I—I take a step back.

ARCHIE: All of us stop cheering, drop arms from the person next to us. Everyone's hugging, smiling. I look up at the hot farmer boy in front of me, whose arms I have been staring at for the past four hours, and he … he smiles at me. I look at the ground.

Beat.

ALL: Sometimes I imagine … another version of myself.

Someone who does things instead of just thinks things.

VIDA: I catch a glimpse of Immi, her face pressed to the window in the van, and for a second, through the crowd, we lock eyes and she presses her hand to the glass.

ARCHIE: I think of Darby and Daniel, their lips separating for the first time in thirty-seven hours; imagine what that must have felt like, a kiss.

CLEM: Banners are resting between people's legs, on their shoulders, all of them with Sofia's face on them, her words: *do something.*

ARCHIE: So I look back into the hot farmer boy's eyes.

CLEM: I look at the megaphone just sitting on the ground, waiting.

VIDA: I look straight at my reflection in the PK's visor.

And it almost catches me off balance

ARCHIE: My knees wobble

CLEM: Fingers tingle

ALL: And I think

VIDA: If you stay, Vida Khan, you will set in motion a series of events that you cannot undo, do you really want to do that?

ALL: I think

CLEM: Do something, Clementine Major, use your voice

ALL: I think

ARCHIE: Uh-oh, Archie Power, you are in trouble.

VIDA: And as the peacekeeper points his capsicum spray right at me, I pull out my phone to film him.

CLEM: I pick up the megaphone, put it to my lips and I begin to chant.

ARCHIE: I smile at Hot Farmer Boy and say *Hey, I'm Archie*.
And I know

VIDA: I know

CLEM: I know, then, that nothing

ARCHIE: Nothing

VIDA: Nothing is going to be the same as it was.

THE END

Melbourne Theatre Company

BOARD OF MANAGEMENT

Jane Hansen AO (Chair)
Tony Burgess
Patricia Faulkner AO
Jonathan Feder
Larry Kamener
Professor Duncan Maskell
Susan Oliver AM
Leigh O'Neill
Professor Marie Sierra
Allan Tait
Anne-Louise Sarks
Virginia Lovett

FOUNDATION BOARD

Jonathan Feder (Chair)
Paul Bonnici
Jennifer Darbyshire
Shane Gild
Jane Grover
Hilary Scott
Tania Seary
Tracey Sisson
Virginia Lovett
Rob Pratt
Rupert Sherwood

EXECUTIVE MANAGEMENT

Artistic Director & Co-CEO
Anne-Louise Sarks
Executive Director & Co-CEO
Virginia Lovett
Executive Assistant
Kathleen Higgs

ARTISTIC

Director of Artistic Operations/Senior Producer
Martina Murray
Associate Director
Petra Kalive
Acting Literary Manager
Jennifer Medway
Casting Director
Janine Snape
Casting Administrator
Carmen Lai
Associate Producer/ Senior Company Manager
Stephen Moore
Company Manager
Julia Smith
Programs Producer
Karin Farrell

DEVELOPMENT

Director of Development
Rupert Sherwood
Annual Giving Manager
Chris Walters
Major Gifts Manager
Sophie Boardley
Philanthropy Coordinator
Emily Jenik
Partnerships Manager
Bella Wren
Partnerships Executive
Alice Fitzgerald

EDUCATION

Head of Education & Families
Jeremy Rice
Learning Manager
Nick Tranter
Digital Content Producer
Bonnie Leigh-Dodds
First Peoples Young Artists Program Administrator
Brodi Purtill
Schools Engagement Officer
Lily Everest

PEOPLE & CULTURE

Director of People & Culture
Sean Jameson
People & Culture Executive
Christine Verginis
Health & Safety Coordinator
Liz Mundell
Receptionist
David Zierk

FINANCE & IT

Director of Finance & IT
Rob Pratt
Finance Manager
Andrew Slee
IT & Systems Manager
Michael Schuettke
IT Support Officer
Darren Snowdon
Payroll Officer
Julia Godinho
Payments Officer
Harper St Clair
Assistant Accountant
Nicole Chong
Building Services Manager
Adrian Aderhold

MARKETING & COMMUNICATIONS

Marketing & Communications Director
Vanessa Rowsthorn
Marketing Manager
Shelley King
Marketing Campaign Managers
Rebecca Lawrence
Ashlee Read
Digital Engagement Manager
Jane Sutherland
Digital Coordinator
Wendy Trieu
Lead Graphic Designer/ Art Director
Kate Francis
Graphic Designer
Helena Turinski
Senior Manager, Communications & External Relations
Rosie Shepherdson-Cullen
Editorial Content Producer
Paige Farrell

TECHNICAL & PRODUCTION

Technical & Production Director
Adam J Howe

PRODUCTION

Senior Production Manager
Michele Preshaw
Production Manager
Michaela Deacon
Production Assistant
Zsuzsa Gaynor Mihaly
Production Administrator
Alyson Brown
Props Buyers/SM Swing
Jess Maguire

TECHNICAL

Technical Manager Lighting & Sound
Kerry Saxby
Senior Production Technician Coordinator
Allan Hirons
Production Technician Coordinator
Nick Wollan
Product Technicians/ Operators
Marcus Cook
Mungo Trumble
Max Wilkie
Technical Manager – Staging & Design
Andrew Bellchambers
CAD Drafter
Jacob Battista
Head Mechanist
Michael Burnell

PROPERTIES

Properties Supervisor
Geoff McGregor
Props Maker
Colin Penn

SCENIC ART

Scenic Art Supervisor
Shane Dunn
Scenic Artist
Colin Harman
Alison Crawford

WORKSHOP

Workshop Supervisor
Andrew Weavers
Deputy Workshop Supervisor
Brian Easteal
Set Makers
Aldo Amenta
Ken Best
Nick Gray
Simon Juliff
Philip de Mulder
Peter Rosa

COSTUME

Costume Manager
Keryn Ribbands
Costume Staff
Jocelyn Creed
Liz Symons
John Van Gastel
Lyn Molloy
Costume Coordinator
Sophie Woodward
Millinery
Phillip Rhodes
Wigs & Makeup
Jurga Celikiene
Costume Hire
Liz Symons

STAGE MANAGEMENT

Christine Bennett
Brittany Coombs
Lisette Drew
Whitney McNamara
Meg Richardson
Jess Maguire
Millie Mullinar
Brodi Purtill
Vivienne Poznanski
Jess Keepence
Pippa Wright

SOUTHBANK THEATRE

Theatre Manager
Mark D Wheeler
Front of House Manager
James Cunningham
Events & Bar Services Manager
Mandy Jones
Production Services Manager
Frank Stoffels
Lighting Supervisor
Geoff Adams
Deputy Lighting Supervisor
Tom Roach
Sound Supervisor
Joy Weng
Fly Supervisor
James Tucker
Deputy Fly Supervisor
Adam Hanley
Stage & Technical Staff
Jon Bargen
Sam Berkley
Max Bowyer
Sam Bruechert
Ash Buchanan
Emily Campbell
Will Campbell
Bryn Cullen
Kit Cunneen
Nathan Evers
Chris Hubbard
Julia Knibbs
Marcus Macris
Alexandre Malta
Scott McAlister
Terry McKibbin
David Membery
Maxwell Murray Lee
Will Paterson
James Paul
Max Wilkie
Tom Willis

HOUSE & BAR SERVICES

House & Bar Supervisors
Tanya Batt
Matt Bertram
Sarah Branton
Kasey Gambling
Daniel Moulds
Paul Terrell
Drew Thomson
House & Bar Attendants
George Abbott
Aisha Aidara
Stephanie Barham
Briannah Borg
Max Bowyer
Zak Brown
Sam Diamond
Leila Gerges
Bear
Hugo Gutteridge
Kathryn Joy
Natasha Milton
Yasmin Mole
Ernesto Munoz
Ben Nichol
Emma Palackic
Sam Perry
Adam Rogers
Sophie Scott
Rain Shadrach
Mieke Singh
Olivia Walker
Alison Wheeldon

TICKETING

Director of Ticketing Operations
Brenna Sotiropoulos
Customer Service Sales Manager
Jessie Phillips
VIP Ticketing Officer
Michael Bingham
Education Ticketing Officer
Mellita Ilich
Subscriptions & Telemarketing Team Leader
Peter Dowd
Subscriptions Ticketing Officers
Dee Wong
Emma Vincin
Isobel Lake
James Meakin
Lily Everest
Lucy Kingsley
Moira Millar
Olivia Brewer
Britt Ferry
Darcy Fleming
Julia Landberg
Box Office Supervisors
Bridget Mackey
Daniel Scaffidi
Box Office Duty Supervisor
Tain Stangret
Box Office Attendants
Sarah Branton
Britt Ferry
Darcy Fleming
Kasey Gambling
Min Kingham
Julia Landberg
Evan Lawson
Julie Leung
Debra McDougall
Lee Threadgold

CRM & AUDIENCE INSIGHTS

Director of CRM & Audience Insights
Jeremy Hodgins
Database Specialist
Ben Gu

COMMISSIONS

The Joan & Peter Clemenger Commissions
Kylie Coolwell
Anthony Weigh
NEXT STAGE Commissions
Van Badham
Carolyn Burns
Angus Cerini
Patricia Cornelius
Tim Finn
Elise Esther Hearst
Andrea James
Phillip Kavanagh
Anchuli Felicia King
Nathan Maynard
Diana Nguyen
Joe Penhall
Leah Purcell
Melissa Reeves
Chris Ryan
Megan Washington
Mark Leonard Winter

OVERSEAS REPRESENTATIVE

New York
Kevin Emrick

Circles of giving

MTC LIFETIME PATRONS

Acknowledging a lifetime of extraordinary support for MTC.

Pat Burke
Peter Clemenger AO and Joan Clemenger AO
Greig Gailey and Dr Geraldine Lazarus
Allan Myers AC QC and Maria Myers AC
The Late Biddy Ponsford
The Late Dr Roger Riordan AM
Maureen Wheeler AO and Tony Wheeler AO
Ursula Whiteside
Caroline Young and Derek Young AM

ENDOWMENT DONORS

Supporting the long term sustainability and creative future of MTC.

Leading Gifts
Jane Hansen AO and Paul Little AO
The Late Max and Jill Schultz
The University of Melbourne

$50,000+
The Late Margaret Anne Brien
Geoffrey Cohen AM
Orcadia Foundation
The Late Biddy Ponsford
Andrew Sisson AO and Tracey Sisson
The John & Myriam Wylie Foundation

$20,000+
Robert A. Dunster
Prof Margaret Gardner AO and Prof Glyn Davis AC
Anne and Mark Robertson OAM

$10,000+
Jane Kunstler
Anonymous

MTC'S PLAYWRIGHTS GIVING CIRCLE

Supporting the NEXT STAGE Writers' Program.

Louise Myer and Martyn Myer AO, Maureen Wheeler AO and Tony Wheeler AO, Christine Brown Bequest
Allan Myers AC QC and Maria Myers AC, Tony Burgess and Janine Burgess
Dr Andrew McAliece and Dr Richard Simmie, Larry Kamener and Petra Kamener

NAOMI MILGROM FOUNDATION

TRUSTS AND FOUNDATIONS

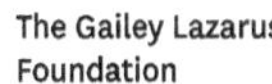

Annual giving

Donors whose recent gifts help MTC enrich and transform lives through the finest theatre imaginable.

Acknowledging Donors who join together to support innovative and inspiring programs for the benefit of our community.

▲ **ARTISTIC DIRECTORS** ○ **PRODUCTION PATRON** ■ **YOUTH AMBASSADORS** ◆ **WOMEN IN THEATRE** ● **EDUCATION**

BENEFACTORS CIRCLE

$50,000+
The Joan and Peter Clemenger Trust
Andrew Sisson AO and Tracey Sisson ○
Maureen Wheeler AO and Tony Wheeler AO

$20,000+
Paul & Wendy Bonnici and Family ●
Krystyna Campbell-Pretty AM ●
Greig Gailey and Dr Geraldine Lazarus
Jane Hansen AO and Paul Little AO ●
Louise and Martyn Myer AO
Janet Reid OAM and Allan Reid
Anne and Mark Robertson OAM ●
Orcadia Foundation ○

$10,000+
Joanna Baevski ○
Erica Bagshaw ◆
Dr Jane Bird ◆
Jill Campbell ○
Kathleen Canfell ○
The Cattermole Family
Chelgrave Contracting Australia PTY LTD ○
Tom and Elana Cordiner ●
Jennifer Darbyshire and David Walker
Linda Herd ● ■
Karen Inge and Dr George Janko
Petra and Larry Kamener
Daryl Kendrick and Sandy Bell
Suzanne Kirkham
Glenda and Greg Lewin AM ○
Macgeorge Bequest
Susanna Mason ▲
Ian and Margaret McKellar
McNeilly Family ○
George and Rosa Morstyn
Helen Nicolay ○
Lisa Ring
Craig Semple ○
Geoff Slade, Slade Group and TRANSEARCH ○
Rob Stewart and Lisa Dowd
Helen Sykes ○
Anita Ziemer ○
Anonymous (6)

$5,000+
Marc Besen AC and Eva Besen AO
James Best and Doris Young
Jay Bethell and Peter Smart
Bill Bowness AO
Dr Andrew Buchanan and Peter Darcy
Ian and Jillian Buchanan
Bill Burdett AM and Sandra Burdett
Lynne and Rob Burgess
Pat Burke and Jan Nolan
Diana Burleigh
The Janet and Michael Buxton Foundation
Dr Anthony Dortimer and Jillian Dortimer
The Dowd Foundation
Prof Margaret Gardner AC and Prof Glyn Davis AC
Nigel and Cathy Garrard
Diana and Murray Gerstman
The Gjergja Family
Henry Gold
Robert and Jan Green
Lesley Griffin
John and Joan Grigg OAM
Jane Hemstritch
Tony Hillery and Warwick Eddington
Bruce and Mary Humphries
Amy and Paul Jasper
Marshall Day Acoustics (Dennis Irving Scholarship)
Dr Andrew McAliece and Dr Richard Simmie
Martin and Melissa McIntosh
Kim and Peter Monk ◆
Jane and Andrew Murray
Peter Nethercote – Ballarat Theatre Company
Tom and Ruth O'Dea ■
Leigh O'Neill ◆
Dr Kia Pajouhesh (Smile Solutions)
Prof David Penington AC and Dr Sonay Hussein
Christopher Reed
Renzella Family
Lynne Sherwood
Tintagel Bay P/L
Trawalla Foundation Trust
The Veith Foundation
Ralph Ward-Ambler AM and Barbara Ward-Ambler
Marion Webster OAM ◆
Ursula Whiteside
Janet Whiting AM and Phil Lukies
J & M Wright Foundation
Anonymous (4)

ADVOCATES CIRCLE

$2,500+
Australian Communities Foundation – Ballandry (Peter Griffin Family) Fund
Ian Baker and Cheryl Saunders
John and Lorraine Bates
Nan Brown
Jenny and Stephen Charles AO
Anne Cleary
Sandy and Yvonne Constantine
Ann Darby ○ ●
Rodney Dux
Dr Justin Friebel and Jessica Rose
Kerry Gardner AM and Andrew Myer AM ○
Gaye and John Gaylard
Heather and Bob Glindemann OAM
Roger and Jan Goldsmith
Fiona Griffiths and Tony Osmond ◆
Jane Grover ◆
Luke Heagerty
Jane Hodder ◆
Peter and Halina Jacobsen
Josephine and Graham Kraehe AO
Joan Lefroy AM and George Lefroy AM
Leg Up Foundation ■
Lording Family Foundation
Virginia Lovett and Rose Hiscock ○
Prof Duncan Maskell
Don and Sue Matthews
Ging Muir and John McCawley ■
Sandy and Sandra Murdoch
Luke and Janine Musgrave
Nelson Bros Funeral Services
Dr Paul Nisselle AM and Sue Nisselle
Bruce Parncutt AO
B & J Rollason
Scanlon Foundation
Hilary and Stuart Scott ●
In memory of Berek Segan AM OBE – Marysia & Marshall Segan ●
Prof Barry Sheehan and Pamela Waller
The Stobart Strauss Foundation
Ricci Swart AM
Richard and Debra Tegoni ● ◆
Anthony Watson and Tracey McDonald
Dr Peter and Dr Carole Wigg
Kaye and John de Wijn
Price and Christine Williams
The Ray and Margaret Wilson Foundation
Gillian and Tony Wood
Anonymous (8)

Annual giving

LOYALTY CIRCLE

$1,000+

Prof Noel Alpins AM and Sylvia Alpins
James Angus AO and Helen Angus
Mary-Louise Archibald
Margaret Astbury
Prof Robin Batterham
Sandra Beanham
Angelina Beninati
Tara Bishop
Judy Bourke
Steve and Terry Bracks AM
Paul and Robyn Brasher
Brett Young Family
Bernadette Broberg
Nigel and Sheena Broughton
Dr Douglas and Treena Brown
Jannie Brown
Beth Brown and the late Tom Bruce AM
Julie Burke
Katie Burke
Hugh Burrill
Pam Caldwell
Alison and John Cameron
John and Jan Campbell
Jessica Canning
Clare and Richard Carlson
Fiona Caro
Chernov Family
Keith Chivers and Ron Peel
Assoc Prof Lyn Clearihan and Dr Anthony Palmer
Dr Robin Collier and Neil Collier
Deborah Conyngham
Ann Cutts
Mark and Jo Davey
Natasha Davies
Katharine Derham Moore
Sandra and Cameron Dorse
Robert Drake
Dr Sally Duguid and Dr David Tingay
Bev and Geoff Edwards
George and Eva Ermer
Anne Evans and Graham Evans AO
Dr Alastair Fearn
Melody and Jonathan Feder
Grant Fisher and Helen Bird
Jan and Rob Flew
Rosemary Forbes and Ian Hocking
Bruce Freeman
Glenn Fryer
John Fullerton
Gill Family Foundation
Charles and Cornelia Goode Foundation
Ian and Wendy Haines
Charles Harkin
Mark and Jennifer Hayes
Kerri Hereward
Dr Alice Hill and Mark Nicholson
Howard and Glennys Hocking
Dr Romayne Holmes
Emeritus Prof Andrea Hull AO
Peter Jaffe and Judy Gold
Ben Johnson
Ed and Margaret Johnson
Leah Kaplan and Barry Levy
Irene Kearsey and Michael Ridley
Malcolm Kemp
Daniel Kilby
Anne and Terry King
Fiona Kirwan-Hamilton and Simon E Marks QC
Doris and Steve Klein
Marianne and Arthur Klepfisz
Larry Kornhauser and Natalya Gill
Alan and Wendy Kozica
Anne Le Huray
Verona Lea
Alison Leslie
Peter and Judy Loney
Lord Family
Kerryn Lowe and Raphael Arndt
Elizabeth Lyons
Chris and Bruce Maple
Ian and Judi Marshman
Margaret and John Mason OAM
Bernie and Virginia McIntosh
Heather and Simon McKeon
Garry McLean
Libby McMeekin
Emeritus Prof Peter McPhee AM and Charlotte Allen
Melman Trading Pty Ltd
Robert and Helena Mestrovic
John G Millard
Ross and Judy Milne-Pott
Patricia Montgomery
MK Futures
Barbara and David Mushin
Brian and Dianne Neilson
Sarah Nguyen
Nick Nichola and Ingrid Moyle
Michele and John Nielsen
David and Lisa Oertle
Susan Oliver AM
In loving memory of Richard Park
Dr Annamarie Perlesz
Peter Philpott and Robert Ratcliffe
Dug and Lisa Pomeroy
Catherine Quealy
Philip and Gayle Raftery
Sally Redlich
Victoria Redwood
Phillip Riggio
Ken Roche
Roslyn and Richard Rogers Family
Dr Paul and Gay Rosen
Paul Ross and Georgina Costello
Jeremy Ruskin and Roz Zalewski
Jenny Russo
Anne and Laurie Ryan
Edwina Sahhar
Margaret Sahhar AM
Lucy and Mathew Saliba
Elisabeth and Doug Scott
Fiona Scott
Sally and Tim Scott
Jacky and Rupert Sherwood
Diane Silk
Dr John Sime
Pauline and Tony Simioni
Jane Simon and Peter Cox
Tim and Angela Smith
Annette Smorgon
Geoff Steinicke
Dr Ross and Helen Stillwell
Helene Strawbridge
Suzy and Dr Mark Suss
James and Anne Syme
Rodney and Aviva Taft
Megan and Damian Thomson
John and Anna van Weel
Valeria Vanselow
Fiona Viney
Graham Wademan and Michael Bowden
Walter and Gertie Wagner
Kevin and Elizabeth Walsh
Pinky Watson
Penelope and Joshua White
Ann and Alan Wilkinson
Mandy and Edward Yencken
Graeme and Nancy Yeomans
Anonymous (53)

LEGACY CIRCLE

Acknowledging supporters who have made the visionary gesture of including a gift to MTC in their will.

John and Lorraine Bates
Mark and Tamara Boldiston
Bernadette Broberg
Adam and Donna Cusack-Muller
Peter and Betty Game
Fiona Griffiths
Linda Herd
Irene Kearsey
Dr Andrew McAliece and Dr Richard Simmie
Libby McMeekin
Peter Philpott and Robert Ratcliffe
Jillian Smith
Diane Tweeddale
Anonymous (14)

Thank you

MTC would like to thank the following organisations for their generous support.

Major Partners

Forum Night & MTC Digital Theatre Partner

Future Directors Initiative Partner

MinterEllison.

Major Marketing Partners

Presenting Partners

THE LANGHAM
MELBOURNE

Associate Partners

Supporting Partners

Marketing Partners

BROADSHEET

CINEMA NOVA

The Monthly
The Saturday Paper
7am

southgate

RRR

Southbank Theatre Partners

CHANDON

THE FRESH COLLECTIVE

mgc
THE MELBOURNE GIN COMPANY

SCOTCHMANS HILL
BELLARINE PENINSULA VICTORIA
ESTABLISHED 1982

To learn more about partnership opportunities at MTC or to host a private event, please contact partnerships@mtc.com.au
Partners current as of March 2022.